THE NATIONAL 3 PEAKS WALK

BEN NEVIS - SCOTLAND
SCAFELL PIKE - ENGLAND
SNOWDON - WALES

ONE BOOK COVERING 3 MOUNTAINS

AN
ESSENTIAL GUIDE TO
HELP YOU COMPLETE
THE
NATIONAL 3 PEAKS WALK

BY
BRIAN G. SMAILES

THE AUTHOR
BRIAN SMAILES

A record was established by him in June 1995 when he completed 5 continuous crossings of the Lyke Wake Walk across the North York Moors in 85hrs 50mins, a total of 210 miles over rough terrain.

Long distance running is one of his interests and he has completed 23 marathons and one 100Km ultra run.

Other achievements include canoeing the Caledonian Canal 3 times and the river Wye, qualified scuba diving instructor and course director for Basic Expedition Leader Award courses.

Brian has travelled extensively around Great Britain and has experience of outdoor pursuits in all conditions.

Books by the same author:-

The Scottish Coast to Coast Walk
ISBN 0-9526900-8-X

The Complete Isle of Wight Coastal Footpath
ISBN 0-9526900-6-3

The Yorkshire Dales Top Ten
ISBN 0-9526900-5-5

John O'Groats to Lands End
ISBN 0-9526900-4-7

The Lakeland Top Ten
ISBN 0-9526900-3-9

**The Novices Guide to the Yorkshire
3 Peaks Walk**
ISBN 0-9526900-0-4

The Novices Guide to the Lyke Wake Walk
ISBN 0-9526900-1-2

ISBN 0-9526900-7-1
First Published 1996
Second Edition 2000

Challenge Publications
7, Earlsmere Drive, Barnsley, S71 5HH

ACKNOWLEDGEMENTS

It is with thanks to the following people that this book has been published:-

Graham Fish - for his help in checking details and advice on topographical matters.
Geoff Whittaker & Janet Crossley - for their help in the research .
Pam Smailes - for her assistance throughout and for accompanying me on this walk.
Pulse 8   - for the fleece clothing. Pulse 8, Wath-upon-Dearne, Rotherham

Photographs by Pam & Brian Smailes, Geoff Whittaker, Janet Crossley.

Brian Smailes is identified as author of this book in accordance with Copyright Act 1988.

First Published 1996
Second Edition 2000

ISBN 0-9526900-7-1

Published by Challenge Publications 7 Earlsmere Drive, Barnsley S71 5HH.
Printed by Dearne Valley Printers, Wath on Dearne, Rotherham.

The information recorded in this book is believed by the author to be correct at time of publication. No liabilities can be accepted for any inaccuracies found. Anyone using this guide should refer to their map in conjunction with this book. The description of a route used is not evidence of a right of way.

CONTENTS

PLATES

Three Peaks Adventure

With all our equipment together
And plans that have taken weeks
We are on our way with confidence
To tackle the National Three Peaks
You can climb them in any order
So armed with map, compass and whistle
We are heading North of the border
Travelling to the land of the thistle
The first mountain we have to conquer
To test the fitness of women and men
Is the highest climb of them all
To reach the summit of The Ben
For the route to the top of Ben Nevis
We will be taking the tourist track
This is the easiest route up there
And it won't take long to get back
We will be up and down Ben Nevis
Just see how long that it takes
Before we are back in Fort William
And heading on down to The Lakes
We are now leaving The Ben behind us
Filled with anticipation we are alike
To go and climb the next mountain
And reach the summit of Scafell Pike
For the next stage of our mission
We are leaving from Wasdale Head
It is a quick and scenic route up there
At least that is what has been said
Then with Scafell Pike now completed
And all safely back down to our wagon
We are on the final stage of our journey
Heading down to the land of the dragon
For the route to the summit of Snowdon
We will take the Pyg or the Miners path
And our legs now tired and aching
Will think of a nice soak in a bath
Then all safely back to Pen-y-Pass
There is one thing we must do
That is give a special thank you
To a wonderful back up crew
Then thank God it was safely completed
And it was not just all a dream
But what made it all possible
Was the help of the back up team

Geoff Whittaker

PREFACE TO THE 2nd EDITION

The routes described in this book are written for walkers who either choose to take up the 3 peaks 24 hour challenge or to climb each peak at a more enjoyable leisurely pace. There is no rule that says you must complete the 3 peaks in 24 hours. Peaks can be climbed over days, weeks or years. Trying to do this in 24 hours leads to loss of enjoyment and a higher risk of accidents.

The effort required to complete the National 3 Peaks cannot be under estimated. The lack of proper sleep, food and comfort takes it's toll on people of all ages particularly those in mid life and over, which is the average age of the long distance walker.

"One of the ultimate challenges in the United Kingdom" is how many people describe this 3 peaks walk. Ben Nevis at 1344m, Scafell Pike at 978m and Snowdon at 1085m. The challenge of climbing the 3 highest mountains in Great Britain appeals to many walkers.

This book looks at preparation, walking and driving routes to use on this classic walk. The inclusion in this edition of campsites and B&B's for each area should prove a valuable help. Sketch maps have been included as a guide to use in conjunction with the relevant map.

The photographs give an accurate representation of the spectacular scenery and the conditions that can be encountered on the 3 peaks walk.

Any compass bearings given in the text are given as magnetic, set in 2000, unless stated.

Following the advice given in this book, which includes new and updated information, should enable all walkers to complete the National 3 Peaks Walk in a safe and competent manner.

It gives me great pleasure to present this 2nd edition of The National 3 Peaks Walk to help you fulfil your ambition.

INTRODUCTION

The National 3 Peaks of Scotland, England and Wales consists of 26 miles of steep rugged ascents and descents.

Thousands of people walk these mountains each year, some only one, others all three. This guide gives you the information you require to complete all 3 peaks safely.

This walk should ideally be attempted between June-Oct, the longest day being 21st June, however it can be done at other times of the year with caution. The weather conditions and darkness can be deciding factors in whether you complete this walk safely. In times of snow the danger of over-hangs, whiteouts and false ledges can all prove fatal if you are ill-prepared. Carry and know how to use essential equipment. In winter an ice axe and crampons are considered essential.

Once you gain the summit of any of these peaks you have an awesome feeling as you look out over the mountains and probably across the low cloud in the valleys and glens. This leaves a lasting impression on any walker of accomplishment that cannot be equalled.

There are well defined paths leading to the summits of Ben Nevis and Snowdon. Scafell Pike is slightly different, the paths are not so well defined in places, but care in planning and on the ascent will help you attain the summit.

The driving route between each mountain is not complicated. Although a suitable route is shown within, drivers can obviously choose their own route which may be more direct or to avoid road works or other congestion.

THE CHALLENGE

In 24 Hours

Start at Loch Linnhe, Fort William by touching the water at the main ferry terminal beside Crannog Sea Food Restaurant. This is near the main car park. Drive 3 miles, heading along Glen Nevis and park near the youth hostel *(plate 2)*. You now follow the route described to the summit of Ben Nevis.

After completing Ben Nevis, head south to either Wasdale Head or Seathwaite in the Lake District. Walk to the summit of Scafell Pike following one of the set routes. You may save some time by following the route from Seathwaite via the Corridor Route to Scafell Pike, returning to Wasdale Head car park *(plate 9)*. This route could save up to 3 hours on the overall journey. My personal preference is to start and finish at Wasdale Head, which I feel is more straightforward, taking only 2¼ hours each way. However many people prefer the other route.

Once you have completed Scafell Pike, head south to Wales. Park at Pen-y-Pass or in Llanberis depending on which walking route you choose. Most people prefer to start from Pen-y-Pass. Ascend to the summit of Snowdon following one of the routes described.

Your 3 peaks challenge is complete when you drive to Caernarfon Castle and touch the water at the side of the castle car park.

When attempting this challenge in 24 hours extra care should be taken because of the increased exertion required to complete in the time limit. Exhaustion can overcome you while on the mountain, then when you stop, even for a short while, hypothermia can become a problem very quickly.

Due to the distance involved, driver fatigue is a major cause of accidents on this challenge.

The Leisurely Alternative

As an alternative to the above challenge the 3 peaks can be walked on 3 individual days, not necessarily consecutive. In choosing this method you will have time to look around Fort William, Keswick, Llanberis or any other of the many tourist attractions on route.

Many people think this walk must be completed in 24 hours, it does not. It is probably a more rewarding experience to take your time and enjoy the once in a lifetime event.

PREPARATION

This walk is not considered long compared with many other walks. Maximum distance on one mountain is 9½ miles, even so if you are not prepared it could lead to problems. In preparing for this walk you need to consider the following:-

FITNESS   FAMILIARISATION
FOOD   EQUIPMENT

Fitness

The main problem on this walk are the steep, rugged ascents and descents especially on Ben Nevis and Scafell Pike. Because of this there is a lot of pressure on the leg muscles, knees and achilles tendon. This pressure will increase considerably if you are attempting to climb the 3 peaks consecutively.

Exercises should be followed to build up stamina i.e. walking, jogging, cycling and swimming all help to improve fitness to attempt this walk.

Some good advice is to pace yourself when ascending each mountain. This will conserve energy and maintain a steady body heat and release of energy. This steady pace will usually help you to overcome steep or difficult sections without becoming exhausted. Some walkers set off at a brisk pace and often become exhausted soon afterwards. The combination of exhaustion and loss of energy can hasten the onset of hypothermia.

Food

The food you consume both before you start and while walking can affect your body heat and energy level. High energy food such as bananas, rice, pasta, potato and wholemeal bread are all carbohydrate rich and of benefit. A high intake of these carbohydrates coupled with a balanced diet of protein, for building body and muscle strength, should give you the strength and energy to complete this walk.

Familiarisation

Study your map and familiarise yourself with the route and various landmarks, where possible visit the areas before you walk. An escape route should be planned in case of bad weather or in the event of an emergency (see bad visibility descents).

When studying your map, note where the mountain rescue posts are situated, along with the nearest telephones and areas where shelter can be provided. Look for danger areas e.g. gullies, ledges etc.

Equipment

Carefully select both personal and safety equipment. Clothing should be capable of keeping you warm and dry. It should protect you from the elements as well as the extreme changes in temperature that occur between the foothills and the summit.

Boots

These are an essential item on this walk. A good fitting pair of boots can make the difference between success or failure on any walk. Ankle protection is important especially on the peaks of Ben Nevis and Scafell Pike where large stones and scree can inflict damage very easily.

Both leather and fabric boots should be waterproofed before use. Most types of leather boots will need 'breaking-in' before use. Regular waxing will help keep the leather soft and supple. A sewn-in tongue will help prevent water and small stones getting into the boot. The addition of 'D' rings and hooks will assist in putting on/taking off the boot. Before buying boots always try them on wearing the socks you will use with them. The boots should not be too tight as to cramp your toes likewise not too slack that your feet move around inside.

Socks

These should be able to keep the feet warm and cushion them from any knocks and constant pounding of the feet. Some walkers prefer to wear 2 pairs of socks, others only one. Whatever your choice they should be approximately 60% wool for good insulating property. Some socks have a thick base to help cushion the feet. You can usually buy short, medium and long depending on preference.

Trousers

Should be loose fitting and ideally made of cotton or a fleece type of material. Cotton trousers will be light to wear, keep you warm and most importantly will dry quickly when wet. Fleece trousers will generally keep you very warm. They are light weight and can be waterproofed.

Jeans are not suitable for walking as they take a long time to dry when wet and become very heavy. They can also chafe the skin, draw the body heat and their insulating property is very low.

Hat

Much of the body's heat is lost through the head, so some protection is strongly advised. Woolly hats were the old favourite, however fleece ones are becoming more popular. Balaclavas are probably better than the traditional hat as they cover the whole head and neck area.

Jacket

Fleece jackets have become very popular over the last few years. If there is a hood attached with a drawstring this will give good protection around the head. Full length two-way zips help to regulate body heat as well as allowing for ease in putting on/taking off while out in a harsh environment.

The addition of numerous pockets, some zipped, provides space for any small items you may like to carry. It is especially beneficial to have a map pocket on the inside. These types of jackets are washable and can be waterproofed to withstand the elements for at least a few hours.

Waterproofs/Windproofs

Jackets which are breathable, waterproof and windproof are becoming very popular, but whichever jacket you are buying make sure it is waterproof and not just showerproof.

Some features to look for on waterproof jackets are:-

• Full length two-way zip to help to regulate body heat and with putting on/taking off. It should also have a flap over it.

• Side pockets also with a flap over to stop water entering.

• Draw-string around the bottom and on the fitted hood.

• Elasticated or adjustable cuffs are essential to stop the wind flow through the jacket.

When buying your jacket make allowance for the other items of clothing you would normally wear underneath and indeed extra items for cold weather.

Waterproof trousers should have an elasticated waist and/or draw-string. Zips on the lower legs are very beneficial as they enable you to put them on/take off without taking your boots off.

Finally all seams on jackets and trousers should be taped to ensure no water passes through. A little candle wax rubbed on the zips will help to keep them running smoothly and keep water out.

Do not wear water/windproofs that are not breathable any longer than necessary as quite often condensation builds up inside. Try to keep the jacket ventilated as much as possible to reduce the condensation.

Gaiters

Help to protect the lower leg from the wet or abrasive rock. Gaiters should be waterproof, ideally breathable, have a hook to attach them to the boots and a full length zip or velcro fastening to enable you to fit them easily.

Gloves

A pair of fleece, woollen gloves or mittens are strongly recommended when ascending the peaks. You will find that 5 finger gloves, as opposed to mittens, are probably better, especially in gale force winds when handling map and adjusting compass and clothing *(plate16)*.

Rucksack

This should be large enough to hold all your personal and safety equipment described. It should be robust enough to stand the test of putting on and removing in all weathers.

A rucksack should ideally have wide padded shoulder straps and a waist belt to stop it moving around. The material may be a type of polyurethane which has been proofed, however it is advisable to put a liner inside to keep your clothes and other items dry in very wet conditions. Most rucksacks have a number of external zipped pockets in which to put small or frequently needed items i.e. water bottle, map, food etc.

The addition of a draw-string to tighten and enclose the items securely from wind, rain and from falling out is helpful and increases the versatility of the rucksack. Quick release plastic clip buckles to open/secure the top are also useful.

In summarising the personal clothing and it's effectiveness on any walker the following points need to be remembered. Clothing should be built up in layers where warm air can be trapped between each one. Three thin sweaters are more effective than one thick one. If you are hot you can easily take a layer off.

Emergency Equipment
This includes spare clothing e.g. sweater, socks etc. which should be carried in the rucksack.

Torch
Each person should carry one, take spare batteries and a bulb. Check it works before each mountain.

Pencil & Notebook
It may be necessary to take notes on route and in an emergency when positions, names, injuries etc. can be written and passed on to emergency services.

Whistle
A plastic whistle should be carried by each person and they should also be familiar with the 'S.O.S.' signal to alert others in times of emergency.

Survival Bag
This is usually made of heavy duty polythene and designed for a walker to get inside to help protect them from the harsh environment and to preserve their body heat. It is a piece of safety equipment which may never be used but should always be carried in your rucksack.

THE BODY

RUCKSACK
Containing food, drinks, first aid, and clothing, map and compass.

THE HEAD
Should be kept warm, more heat is lost from the head than anywhere else.

THE BODY
*Should be kept warm.
Build clothes up in layers with wind/waterproofs on top.*

HANDS
Should be kept warm with gloves.

MAIN BODY CORE
Temperature must be maintained.

LEGS
It is important not to wear jeans

ANKLES
Should be protected by wearing boots. These will help stop you going over on your ankle and strengthen it.

FEET
Should be kept well cushioned and dry if possible. Good fitting boots will help prevent blisters

Plate 5

16

FIRST AID

A knowledge of basic first aid would be helpful on any walk. To be able to bandage cracked ribs, put a sling on or dress a wound can be vital in times of accidents especially on the peaks when hypothermia can set in.

In any accident or emergency situation the ability to reassure the casualty and comfort them is very important, do not move the casualty if the accident is of a possible serious nature e.g. a back or head injury. Keep the casualty warm and reassured, then send for help. Someone should stay with the injured person. If the injury is not of a serious nature the injured person should, if and when possible, be removed from danger.

The possibility of shock or delayed shock can present further problems for the casualty so reassurance and company is vital as well as getting down the mountain to safety.

It is a fact that the majority of accidents happen on the return or second half of the journey. This is probably due to fatigue, cold, tiredness or complacency. Be aware and alert throughout the walk to possible dangers.

Common Types of Injuries

Cuts and grazes   *Broken Arms/Legs*
Blisters   *Cracked Ribs*
Hypothermia   *Head Injuries*
Sprained Ankle/Wrist   *Gashed Shins*

All the above, however minor, can prove fatal with the casualty going into shock, especially on an exposed area of the mountain or in times of panic, fog or adverse conditions, coupled with the injury.

Walk in small groups of 4-6 people where possible and be aware. If anyone is badly injured then 2 people should go for help, this should be the fittest person and the best navigator. They should take their own personal safety equipment with them. The rest of the group should stay with the injured person to help and reassure them.

Individual First Aid Kit

Adhesive Dressing	*Waterproof Container*
Triangular Bandage	*Sterile Dressing*
Bandage	*Crepe Bandage*
Safety Pins	*Gauze/Lint*
Scissors	*Micropore*
Insect Repellent	*Sun Cream*

Leaders First Aid Kit

A Gregsons First Aid Kit is available from outdoor shops and is recommended for group walks.

HYPOTHERMIA

Hypothermia is caused when the body core temperature falls below 35°C. If a walker is not properly prepared for the conditions or the equipment/clothing is not satisfactory then a combination of the cold, wet, exhaustion and the wind chill factor can give a walker hypothermia.

The Signs and Symptoms in Descending Order:-

Shivering
Cold, pale and dry skin
Low body temperature
Irrational behaviour
A gradual slip into unconsciousness
Pulse and respiratory rate slow
Difficulty in detecting breathing and pulse when unconscious
Death

Ways of Preventing Hypothermia

1. Build up body clothing in thin layers, adding on or taking off as necessary.
2. Have suitable wind/waterproofs with you.
3. Take some food/hot drink or boiled sweets which produce energy and heat during digestion.
4. Wear a balaclava/woolly hat to insulate the head, and some gloves *(plate 16)*.
5. Shelter out of the wind.
6. Take a survival bag and if conditions dictate, use it.

In any type of emergency/accident situation it is always advisable to come off the mountain as soon as possible especially in fog, snow or other bad conditions. The temperature difference between the valley and the summit can be several degrees. If the injured walker is able to move safely, going down the mountain is usually the best solution.

When conditions do not permit movement and if you are in a sheltered area, stay where you are until such time as conditions improve. It may be at this time that you put on extra clothing and use survival bags.

Treatment for Hypothermia

1. Provide extra clothing and shelter from the elements.
2. Bodily warmth of others helps in a gradual warming.
3. If well enough come down into a warmer sheltered area.
4. Give hot drinks if conscious.
5. Give chocolate or sweets if the patient can still take food.
6. The casualty should be placed so that the head is slightly lower than the body.

DO NOT *rub the skin or use a hot water bottle as this can cause a surge of blood from the central body core to the surface, this could prove fatal.*

Alcohol should not be consumed on any walk and should not be given to anyone who has hypothermia. The body temperature will be lowered as well as giving a false sense of security.

MOUNTAIN SAFETY

Details of your route should be left with your support team or someone who can monitor your progress and most importantly alert the rescue services if you are overdue. Because you plan a route it does not mean you have to use it. It is better to cancel if there is a problem than to risk lives ascending a mountain in atrocious conditions or badly prepared.

Many people do not realise that a calm sunny day in the valley can mean low cloud and gale force winds on the summit, add to this the wind chill factor and a badly prepared walker has got problems *(plate 14).* Bad weather can sweep in quickly.

Only walk routes which are within the capability of your party. One of the most common problems that leads to accidents is walkers becoming separated from each other. There should be a party leader and that person should ensure the group walks at a sensible pace. This is usually the speed of the slowest walker. Each person should carry a map and compass and know how to use them. A route card should be carried by each person and they should all have been involved in drawing up the route before hand.

If you are delayed e.g. you have descended into the wrong valley, inform your base or the police as quickly as possible to avoid the mountain rescue team from being called out unnecessarily.

All walkers should be familiar with the
INTERNATIONAL DISTRESS SIGNAL

6 long blasts on whistle
6 shouts or waves of handkerchief
6 flashes of torch in succession
All followed by a pause of one minute, then repeated.

A red flare is a distress signal.

You may at some time have to pass on an emergency message to police. You should have all the information written down to help ensure the right details are passed on to the emergency services.

These are:-
* Name and age of casualty
* Nature of injuries
* Location with 6 figure grid reference and description of area around them
* Time of accident
* Details of the rest of the party with colours of clothing worn
* Where you are calling from and your name and address

The Mountain Code

* Select equipment carefully
* Learn how to use it
* Be physically fit
* Know how to use a map and compass
* Where possible make an early start allowing time later in the day for bad weather
* If possible plan an alternative route for bad weather
* Keep together
* Fill in route card and give a copy to the support team.
* Check weather forecast

THE COUNTRY CODE

The countryside is a place where many people like to escape to and enjoy at various times. To do this we need to look after it when we use it and to preserve it for future generations.

The following is a simple lists of do's and don'ts to help everyone enjoy the countryside.

Do
- Guard against all risk of fire
- Fasten all gates
- Keep dogs under close control
- Use gates and stiles to cross walls and fences
- Protect wildlife, trees and plants
- Take litter home
- Leave nothing but footprints, take nothing but photographs
- Be conscious at all times of erosion of footpaths

Don't
- Play radios etc. or create unnecessary noise
- Take mountain bikes on walkways
- Touch machinery, livestock or crops

WEATHER FORECASTS

The importance of predicting the weather pattern before you ascend each peak can be vital to the success or failure of you and your team.

Notices displaying the current weather patterns on the peaks of Ben Nevis and Snowdon are usually near the start of the routes described. It is advisable to listen to the forecast on local radio if possible for the area you are in.

Calm, still weather in the valley or glen can be gale force winds on the peaks. Check your forecast before you ascend, are you liable to encounter low cloud, heavy rain, snow or scorching sun on your journey? Usually the forecast can help in deciding what and how much extra clothing you need to take with you and equally whether you need suntan cream, insect repellent and extra fluid.

It is essential not only to listen to the forecast but to write it down and remember it. You can then plan your day to make the best use of the winds and your walking time e.g. a circular walk or walking with the wind behind you.

When walking in mountainous country you can often tell if there is or will be a deterioration in the weather by the onset of low cloud around the peaks. Before this happens check your present position and look in the direction you are intending to go as far as you can see. Take a bearing with your compass then follow that bearing through the cloud to your intended destination using both map and compass where necessary. Never be caught unawares, when you reach that spot look again as far as you can see, take your bearing again then proceed as before.

On the National 3 Peaks snow can present problems at certain times of the year *(plate 8)*. Whiteout conditions are created by 'driving' snow. Where conditions are very bad then only those with a great amount of experience should be on the mountains. In virtually every type of situation like this it is better to abandon the attempt than to risk lives on dangerous peaks.

NAVIGATION

The ability to find your way from one place to another especially in bad weather is something that needs to be learned. Although we may have a sixth sense or sense of direction, when the fog closes in even the best of us can get lost quickly.

Before embarking on your 3 Peaks walk you should have an understanding of the basic principles of map reading and compass use. It is not intended that this walking guide should give you the information on how to use navigational equipment but only to point out the need for walkers to be prepared before venturing out especially in bad visibility.

Learning how to read the contours of a map as well as being able to recognise landmarks can only be of benefit. Combine this with basic course plotting and magnetic variation to help you to come down from the mountain in any problem situation.

There is a need to practice your navigation skills until you feel confident enough to venture onto the hills and moorland. Most people know the general principles of pilotage where the sun rises in the east and sets in the west, you can therefore get some idea on a clear day as to which general direction you are walking in, however you would not know if you were heading into danger e.g. steep gullies, cliffs or overhangs.

There are many books that deal with map and compass training, courses are available to those that seek them. Use and learn as much as possible about map and compass work.

GRID REFERENCES

As a walker you will find it necessary at some time to either find a place from a given grid reference or to make a grid reference from a place on a map.

All maps have grid lines running north/south and east/west. These are called 'Eastings' and 'Northings' and these lines have numbers on them. They can be further split into tenths, the numbers range from 00 to 99.

Grid references are normally given in six figures. The first three figures indicate how far to the east the place is. The second three figures indicate how far to the north the place is.

When making a grid reference look from left to right on your map and read the numbers going from left to right. Write down the numbers for the grid line to the left of your position, estimate the tenths to your position and write that number down to make 3 numbers.

Now look up your map and write the 2 numbers from the line just below your position. Repeat the second sequence as above. You should now have 6 numbers.

Grid references are usually written as G.R. 647556.

In using this method you should be able to pinpoint your target or position quite accurately on a 1:25000 scale map. Before you ascend the peaks you need to practise until you can both find grid reference points on a map and create a grid reference from a given position e.g. the grid reference for Ben Nevis is 167713 at the observatory using 6 figures and on map 38 of the O.S. Outdoor Leisure Series.

Plate 1
Ben Nevis as viewed from Corpach - Snow on the summit can last into July.

Plate 2
Looking towards Glen Nevis, the start from the Youth Hostel can be seen.
The alternative path can be seen mid right joining the main path up from the Youth Hostel.

29

GLEN NEVIS AREA

Fort William is the main town near the foothills of Ben Nevis. It also represents the start or end of the Caledonian Canal which runs to Inverness on the east coast *(plate 1)*.

Within the area there are many guest houses and outdoor activity centres which cover all manner of water sports and land based activities.

A tourist information centre in Fort William provides interesting displays of local attractions as well as general information about the area. The Glen Nevis Visitor Centre also gives information, especially on Ben Nevis.

There are many mountains situated in the area, whisky distilleries to visit, cable cars and cruises to venture on. Local restaurants around Fort William offer good food.

Many of the buildings are stone built and the town is clean and pleasant. The local people are keen to welcome visitors and there are numerous hostelries in which to sample local ale. A visit into the town is not to be missed. There are a number of outdoor shops selling maps, compasses and most outdoor equipment.

Loch Linnhe borders Fort William and provides good fishing and sailing for those who enjoy alternative sports and hobbies. Those walkers who have time to relax after climbing Ben Nevis will find the area around Fort William very pleasant and picturesque. A wide range of shops cater for all tastes in local food and souvenirs.

Travelling to Fort William by car will give some of the best views anywhere in the U.K. particularly travelling through Glen Coe. A rail and bus link will transport you there from throughout the British Isles. Take a camera to give you some lasting memories.

The path to the summit of Ben Nevis was originally built as a pony track to service the observatory and the hotel which are now in ruins *(plate 7)*. The observatory was operational between 1883-1904. The highest war memorial in Britain is also situated on this summit. The views from here are breathtaking in all directions.

The tourist path is used for the Ben Nevis annual race which usually takes place on the first Saturday in September. It is supervised by the Lochaber mountain rescue team.

The road along Glen Nevis runs for approximately 7 miles. You will find the visitor centre, the Glen Nevis Caravan & Camping Park and the youth hostel along this road. The mountains tower on both sides of the glen where you must eventually stop at a car park at the far end.

Plate 3

View of Lochan Meall an t Suidhe showing the route in the foreground with Loch Eil at the top.

Plate 4
View showing the difficulty walking route on Ben Nevis

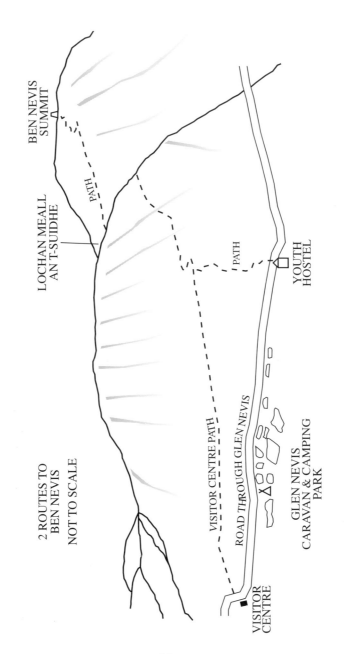

2 ROUTES TO
BEN NEVIS
NOT TO SCALE

BEN NEVIS
SUMMIT

LOCHAN MEALL
AN T-SUIDHE

PATH

PATH

YOUTH
HOSTEL

VISITOR CENTRE PATH

ROAD THROUGH GLEN NEVIS

GLEN NEVIS
CARAVAN & CAMPING
PARK

VISITOR
CENTRE

BEN NEVIS

There are 2 main starting points to climb Ben Nevis - The Youth Hostel and the Glen Nevis Visitor Centre.

Start A - Youth Hostel

Start by touching the water of Loch Linnhe beside Crannog Sea Food Restaurant, near the main car park in Fort William. It is also the main ferry terminal. Take the Inverness road, a sign at the Nevis Bridge roundabout points across to Glen Nevis. Pass Glen Nevis Caravan and Camping Park and park near the telephone box by the youth hostel (limited parking). This is 2.1 miles from the roundabout.

Your ascent of Ben Nevis begins here *(plate 2)*. Immediately opposite the youth hostel there is a footbridge, cross it, then cross some steps over a fence. A sign here should display a description of Ben Nevis with the current weather forecast and other information.

Continue up a winding, stony path, a man made path develops forming steps as you ascend. Part way up the path joins another path from your left *(plate 2)* (this path is from the alternative start at Glen Nevis Visitor Centre).

Start B - Glen Nevis Visitor Centre

Start by touching the water as 'A' then from the roundabout it is 1.2 miles to the Glen Nevis Visitor Centre. Park in the free car park here. Near the car park is a pedestrian suspension bridge crossing the River Nevis. A sign points to Ben Path.

Plate 6
The final push to the summit of Ben Nevis

Plate 7
Ben Nevis summit showing the emergency shelter, triangulation pillar and
the ruins of the observatory. (Summer conditions)

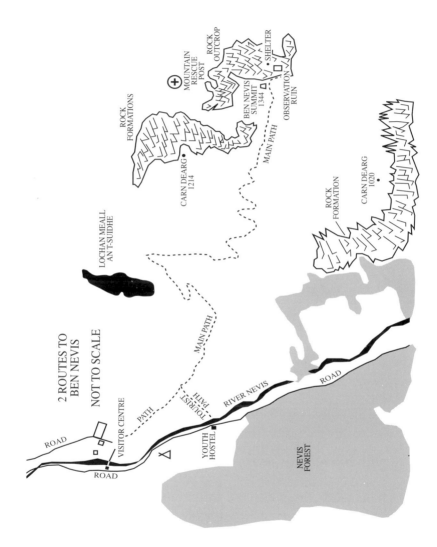

2 ROUTES TO BEN NEVIS

NOT TO SCALE

ROAD

ROAD

VISITOR CENTRE

PATH

TOURIST PATH

MAIN PATH

YOUTH HOSTEL

RIVER NEVIS

ROAD

NEVIS FOREST

LOCHAN MEALL AN T-SUIDHE

ROCK FORMATIONS

CARN DEARG 1214

MOUNTAIN RESCUE POST

ROCK OUTCROP

SHELTER

BEN NEVIS SUMMIT 1344

OBSERVATION RUIN

MAIN PATH

ROCK FORMATION

CARN DEARG 1020

Follow this passing Achintee Guest House and Farm. The visitor centre is now opposite. A sign states Ben Path going over 3 wooden steps. Ascend for 150m then over 2 steps, going straight ahead. As you ascend you have a good view of Glen Nevis Caravan & Camping Park behind you. The path is stony, uneven and ascends steeply. Continue on this path which soon joins path 'A'.

Both paths converge and you cross over a wooden platform bridge. You are now on the main path ascending Ben Nevis which is known as The Tourist Route. The path is very stony and more uneven on this section. Approximately 80m further up is a seat on a bend in the path. You come to a metal bridge and this point affords good views of Glen Nevis.

Cross over a small burn running down a gully, the path here is hard mud, interspersed with stones as it winds up the hillside. The path turns sharp left then right, followed by steps up a steep rock outcrop. A metal bridge spans a gully, again there are good views. The sound of a fast flowing burn running down another gully can be heard. A natural spring escapes from the hillside so the path is usually wet here.

A stone outcrop and another metal bridge with a waterfall beneath is crossed. The path then ascends steeply . You ascend between the two mountains with a burn on your right. It is called Red Burn in English. While ascending the side of the mountain burn you come to a sign saying Conservation Area. The path twists left and right as you approach the small loch halfway up the mountain.

Plate 8
Ben Nevis - The Triangulation Pillar and the roof of Great Britain.
Note - The snow overhang and gully, mid-right.

Plate 9
Wasdale Head car park with Scafell Pike above.

41

The path levels out a little here with springs and melting snow making it wet in places. The area is open with a large expanse of grass. Lochan Meall an t-Suidhe is on the left *(plate 3).*

Follow the path as it turns right and uphill again *(plate 4).* Some piles of stones mark the path. Go immediately right at the second pile of stones. It is important to note that the path going straight on leads to the area the climbers use.

Cross a small stream which runs down the path. There are good views over the other mountains. To your right there is a steep drop over the edge. Cross over another burn where walkers usually stop for refreshment. Approaching the summit you can see down the glen to the youth hostel. Loch Linnhe is in the distance *(plate 6).*

The final ascent is very rocky and uneven, with loose stone and scree. As you approach a gully the route bends sharp right on the scree path. You should see the mountain rescue hut 400m away in front. Near the summit the path levels out, with a lot of small stones. Quite often, up to mid summer, this area is covered in snow.

The mountain rescue hut is now to your left and the path you take bears right to the summit. If there is no snow you should see piles of stones as you proceed on your ascent. Follow your path carefully if there is snow, it is important to stay on the path.

Immediately before the summit take extreme care of the sheer drops over the edge of the mountain, down the infamous Gardyloo Gully, Tower Gully and No.2 Gully *(plate 8)*. Stay on the path watching for snow overhangs which can be deceiving *(plate 8)*. The gully just before the flat plateau summit is close to the path, so keep right, heading for the ruins of the observatory *(plate 7)* which date back to Victorian Times.

On reaching the summit you have excellent views in all directions (cloud permitting). There is a triangulation pillar, number S1595 *(plate 8)* and emergency shelter *(plate 7)*. A cross with a cairn and plaque states it is Britain's highest War Memorial. It is the Fort William Dudley/Worcestershire Cairn of Remembrance.

After resting for a short time on the summit you may find the cold penetrating the body. This is now the time to start your descent to warmer and more sheltered areas. Retrace your steps down the mountain following the route you ascended.

In times of bad visibility follow the bearings and directions given in the chapter on bad visibility descents. N.B. Ben Nevis should be treated with respect at all times, at over 4,000ft the weather on top can be very different to what you expect e.g. deep snow in May *(plate 8)*, thick fog and ice. It is advisable to carry good quality maps of Ben Nevis with bad visibility routes in scales of 1:10,000 or better. This is for your safety and that of others.

Plate 10
Path ascending to Brown Tongue on route to Scafell Pike.

Plate 11

Walkers on route to Scafell Pike with Wastwater in the background. Note: the stony and uneven path.

45

DRIVING ROUTE TO SCAFELL PIKE

	Road	Destination
Leave Fort William	**A82**	North Ballachulish
at North Ballachulish	**A82**	Crianlarich via Rannoch Moor
at Crianlarich	**A82**	Tarbet
at Tarbet	**A82**	Dumbarton
at Dumbarton	**A82**	Erskine Toll Bridge
at Erskine Toll Bridge	**M898**	Glasgow
at Bridge (south)	**M8**	M74
on M74	**M74**	Abington
at Abington	**A74M**	Gretna
at Gretna	**A74**	Carlisle
at Carlisle	**M6**	Penrith
at Penrith	**A66**	Keswick
at Keswick	**B5289**	Grange
at Grange	**B5289**	Seatoller
at Seatoller	**Minor**	Seathwaite
Leave Walkers		Drive to Wasdale Head for pick-up
at Seathwaite	**B5289**	Crummock Water
at Crummock Water	**B5289**	Brackenthwaite
at Brackenthwaite	**Minor**	Mockerkin Tarn A5086
Mockerkin Tarn	**A5086**	Egremont
at Egremont	**A595**	Gosforth
at Gosforth	**Minor**	Wellington
at Wellington	**Minor**	Wastwater
at Wastwater	**Minor**	Wasdale Head

Park in the car park just past the northern end of Wastwater at the side of the campsite (charge).

Should you decide to pick up and drop off from Wasdale Head then insert section of A66 between Keswick and Cockermouth into your route while referring to your map.

SCAFELL AREA

Scafell Pike is bordered by Wastwater on the south western side of the Lake District and Derwentwater to the north. The nearest main towns are situated several miles away, Keswick, Cockermouth and Ambleside are all within easy reach by car.

There are numerous small villages all round the area with the occasional shop or public house. Picnic areas abound throughout the Lake District especially around the lakes themselves. Birds and other wildlife are plentiful. Scafell Pike is in the heart of the largest national park in England which has 16 lakes within it's area. Much of the area is owned by the National Trust.

When ascending Scafell Pike from Seathwaite via the Corridor Route, ample parking can be found in Seathwaite. You arrive there by passing Grange at the southern end of Derwentwater. There is a café at Seathwaite and a trout farm. The scenery all around the area is very picturesque.

Approaching Scafell foothills from Wastwater there is a large car park (charge) *(plate 9)* and a campsite together at the northern end of the lake. Here is the start of the walk. Continuing up the road, past the end of the lake, you will find Wasdale Head Hotel. Next to it is an outdoor shop which has a campsite opposite it. All around here is mountainous with spectacular scenery.

Plate 12

Crossing the beck with Brown Tongue, centre, Scafell Pike, top and walkers path extreme right.

Plate 13
Scafell Pike ahead, walk around the rock outcrop on the left
of the Pike then ascend.

On the final approach to the summit of Scafell Pike you will see Great Gable with Sty Head Tarn below and Derwentwater in the distance *(plate 15)*. This is the general direction of the Corridor Route. Looking the opposite way you see Wastwater back down in the valley. During darkness you can often see Wastwater and it's reflection. This will give you an unmistakable point to aim for on your descent during darkness. Take care to pick out your path carefully on a night descent. The route from Wasdale to the summit during darkness is by far the easiest to walk and navigate.

The first sections of the walk from Seathwaite via the Corridor Route to the summit are good but it becomes progressively more difficult as you proceed.

Whichever route you choose pick out your path carefully, use your map and compass wisely and accurately.

Take your waterproofs with you when visiting Seathwaite. *This is the wettest place in Great Britain!*

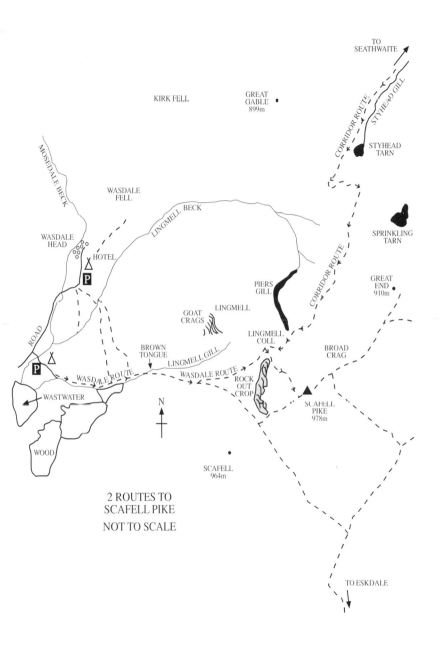

TO
SEATHWAITE

KIRK FELL

GREAT
GABLE •
899m

MOSEDALE BECK

WASDALE
FELL

LINGMELL BECK

WASDALE
HEAD

HOTEL

CORRIDOR ROUTE

STYHEAD GILL

STYHEAD
TARN

SPRINKLING
TARN

GREAT
END •
910m

PIERS
GILL

CORRIDOR ROUTE

GOAT
CRAGS

LINGMELL

LINGMELL
COLL

BROAD
CRAG

ROAD

BROWN
TONGUE

LINGMELL GILL

WASDALE ROUTE

WASDALE ROUTE

ROCK
OUT
CROP

SCAFELL
PIKE
978m

WASTWATER

N

WOOD

SCAFELL
964m

2 ROUTES TO
SCAFELL PIKE

NOT TO SCALE

TO ESKDALE

51

Plate 14
Scafell Pike - Extreme conditions just off the summit.
Wind chill factor -12°C.

Plate 15 - View from Scafell Pike looking to Sty Head Tarn.
The path leading back to Seathwaite is just visible beyond the tarn. Derwent Water is in centre background.

53

SCAFELL PIKE - via Wasdale Head

Approach on the undulating road alongside Wastwater. A sign points to Wasdale Head. Turn right over the stone packhorse bridge. A car park (charge) is at the side of the campsite at the end of Wastwater *(plate 9)*. Your ascent of Scafell Pike begins here. A compass bearing from the car park looking directly to Scafell Pike is 98° magnetic.

Turn left out of the car park and walk up the stony farmers road. Cross over a wooden bridge where the beck flows into Wastwater 100m to the right. Turn left where a small wooden sign points to Eskdale, then up the right side of the beck.

Near the house another small sign says 'Permissive Path, Scafell' which passes the left side of the house.

About 100m from the house is another bridge for walkers only which crosses the small stream. Cross, then go through a gate, follow the path upwards.

A sign states 'National Trust Property' and is next to a kissing gate. Go through onto a narrow path, this is stony in places, winding it's way up the mountain between the bracken on your left and the beck on your right. The path ascends steeply in places and numerous large rocks cover the path *(plate 10)*.

Looking back you can see Wastwater and the Irish Sea in the background beyond Workington Power Station *(plate 11)*. Scafell Pike is the sheer cliffs you can see directly ahead at the top of the valley *(plate 9)*. Pass through another kissing gate with the beck still on the right. Continue up the very stony path.

A compass bearing taken just before Brown Tongue and in direct line to the Pike reads 98°m. You now come to a shorter stretch of man made cobbled path which is easier to walk on. You can now see Brown Tongue where you ascend the right side *(plate 12)*. There is another section of cobbled path with a pile of stones formed into a cairn.

You now cross the beck at the foot of Brown Tongue, you will see the path across the far side of the beck *(plate 12)*. Ascend the cobbled path alongside another beck.

A small cairn marks a fork in the path, take the left path into heather and peat. The path turns stony soon after. You can see the path ahead but in parts it is not so well defined *(plate 13)*. The ground is flatter here with grass and lots of stones scattered around.

There is a scree slope leading to Mickledore to the right between the Pike and Scafell itself. It is a shorter route to the top but more dangerous to ascend or descend the scree slope, especially at night.

Small cairns mark the main path which is small stone and shale with grass on both sides. There is a stone outcrop to the left side of the Pike

Plate 16

Enjoying walkers cake on Scafell summit. Note : Gloves, hood and windproof.

Plate 17
View of Llyn Padarn or Llanberis Lake with the
Llanberis path in the foreground.

(plate 13). Skirt around the left side of it, look for small cairns. Walk in a semi-circle to the large stone outcrop, then look carefully to the right for the cairns on the final ascent to the Pike.

Much of the remaining section consists of large stones which you must walk over *(plate 14).* One slip and you could break an ankle between the stones, so take care here. Look to your left as you ascend, you should see Sty Head Tarn which is near to the beginning of the Corridor Route to Scafell Pike from Seathwaite. Beyond this tarn is Derwent Water *(plate 15).*

On gaining the summit *(plate 16)* there is a triangulation pillar and a wind shelter. Views from the summit include the Scottish Borders, Blackpool, Windermere and on a clear night the lights of Douglas on the Isle of Man can be seen.

On this as on any mountain peak it can be very cold with gale force winds. The wind chill factor should be taken seriously, so windproof clothing needs to be worn before reaching the summit *(plate 16).*

On the return journey down the mountain pick out the path carefully especially in the dark. In the event of low cloud or loss of bearings, follow the bad visibility descent detailed in this book. On a dark clear night the reflection of Wastwater is usually very evident and should help to point you in the general direction of Wasdale Head.

SCAFELL PIKE - via Seathwaite,
(Corridor Route)

When you arrive at Seathwaite there is parking available near the farm. Nearby is a small café and a trout farm. Your ascent via the Corridor Route to Scafell Pike starts here.

As you start walking you go through a farm gate, continue on the path. Follow the path going over a stile next to a gate, into the distance up the valley. Cross a small wooden bridge over the river. The path starts to ascend as you go into the head of the valley. Following the course of the stream you come to a gate and stile. The path is undulating.

Cross the small but impressive stone packhorse bridge which is in front. When you pass through the gate the path starts to ascend steeply. Go through a small gate between a stone wall, the obvious path bears off to the right.

Looking back at night towards Seathwaite you can often see a small light at the farm. This is a guide for any walkers returning at night by this route, especially in bad weather.

Approaching the head of the valley the path flattens a little. A waterfall runs on your right and the path becomes very uneven and turns slightly left between the head of the two hills. It is very important to keep the beck on your right because in extreme weather conditions there is a tendency to walk to the higher ground on the left then cross the beck onto the right side which is damp and boggy.

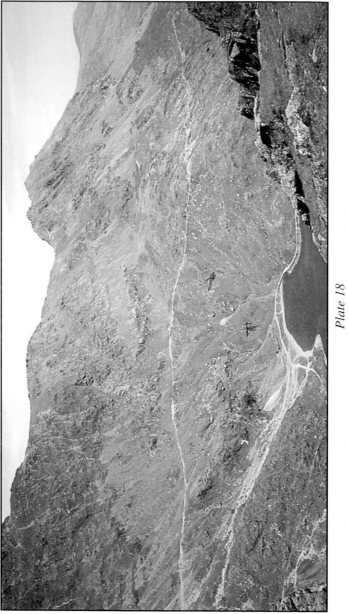

Plate 18

The ridge of Crib Goch with the Pyg track in centre and Miners track at the bottom
showing decent from the Pyg track to the Miners track

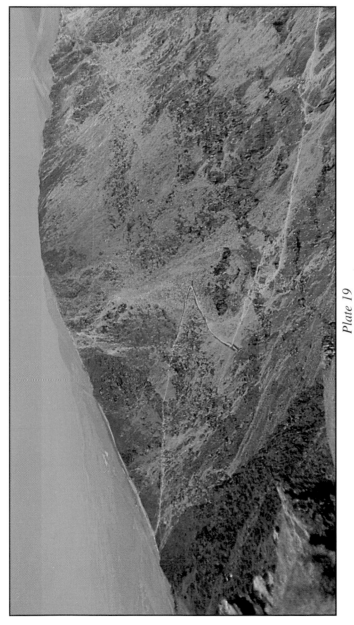

Plate 19

View of the final section of the Pyg track to the Monolith on Snowdon Ridge, showing zig-zag path.

The path along by the beck is very uneven with large stones and is difficult to walk over. There is a cairn on the level area between the two hills. It may be surrounded by water in extreme conditions but is a good route marker. The cairn is approximately 80m from the wooden bridge you see in front following the rough uneven path. Cross the bridge.

The path is now on the right of the beck. In bad conditions it can be very wet. Walk up between the hills to another cairn on your left. Just past it cross the beck again still following the main path. There is a tarn on your left side called Sty Head Tarn *(plate 15)*. Cross over another beck, the path is now better to walk on.

The path starts to divide nearing the head of the valley, it is important to head for the large rocks you see in front of you, the path in parts here is grass. You come to a mountain rescue first aid stretcher box.

To this point the paths are reasonably obvious to see and follow but from here the route becomes difficult to see, walk along and navigate. Take great care and constantly refer to map and compass.

Past the big stone you bear left descending slightly and crossing over some marshy ground. You then rise up again over a grass area then drop down to the foot of the mountain which is straight in front of you. A magnetic bearing of 150°m from the stretcher box should take you across and up the side of the mountain along the Corridor Route.

Pick up a distinct path up the hillside which is very steep in places with a drop off to your right. Looking down the valley you can see Wastwater. The path winds it's way to the summit but first it leads down and around to the left where there is a small cairn. The area is extremely steep and CARE should be taken. Go around the side of the waterfall known as Piers Gill. You pass another small cairn and some large rocks which you walk between as you near the summit.

On the path there is a ravine with a waterfall. You need to be careful where you are stepping. There is another distinct waterfall coming over the edge on the right with a steep drop down. Keep in to the left side of the path.

You emerge at the foot of Scafell Pike at the base of Lingmell Col. The remaining section has large stones to walk over. Take care not to loose your footing, look for piles of stones marking the route to the summit.

It is left to you the reader to decide which route to choose. I prefer to walk up and return on the Wasdale/Wastwater route. This route is probably better for those who are not extremely skilled in map reading and using a compass. The Corridor Route is not recommended at night and especially in bad conditions. Once on the summit, if conditions are bad, follow the bad visibility descent detailed in this book.

Plate 20
View to Llyn Llydaw reservoir showing Pyg track on left and Miners track around reservoir.

64

Plate 21
Pyg track ascending to Snowdon with low cloud behind.

DRIVING ROUTE TO SNOWDON

	Road	**Destination**
Leave Car Park	**Minor**	Santon Bridge
at Stanton Bridge	**Minor**	Holmrook
at Holmrook	**A595**	Broughton in Furness
at Broughton	**A5092**	Haverthwaite
at Haverthwaite	**A590**	J36 of M6
J36 of M6	**M6**	M56 Chester
M56	**M56**	Queensferry A494
at Queensferry	**A55**	Llandudno Junction
at Llandudno J'tion	**A470**	Betws-y-Coed
at Betws-y-Coed	**A5**	Capel Curig
at Capel Curig	**A4086**	Pass of Llanberis

Park in the main car park at Pen-y-Pass near the youth hostel (charge made).

The distance by road is approximately 470 miles, depending on which driving route you choose. Total drive time is about 10½ hours. It is recommended that drivers are changed regularly to avoid driver fatigue. Care should be taken to observe the speed limits. It is better to reach your destination intact than not at all.

SNOWDON AREA

Mount Snowdon is situated in the Snowdonia National Park, covering an area of 840 square miles. The area around Snowdon is very mountainous as you would imagine. The views all around the region are good and there are some picturesque villages within a short travelling distance.

The main recommended route is situated in the pass of Llanberis where it meets with Pen-y-Pass. There is a youth hostel here and a mountain rescue post. Near Pen-y-Pass there are a number of small lakes or tarns. The largest Llyn Llydaw is a reservoir *(plate 20).*

The town of Llanberis is 6 miles away on the shore of Llyn Padarn or Llanberis Lake. Along the shore of this lake is a steam railway which is open to visitors. Probably the most famous tourist attraction in this area is the Snowdon Mountain Railway. This line starts in Llanberis and continues to the summit of Snowdon. It is Britains only rack and pinion mountain railway.

On the summit there is a café and gift shop where thirsty walkers can quench their thirst and purchase souvenirs. Some walkers prefer to travel one way on the railway and the other on foot.

Throughout the area there are many tourist attractions but to do justice to them you need to spend a number of days exploring, walking and visiting all that the Snowdon area has to offer (see section on attractions). A few miles away is Betws-y-Coed and Caernarfon which are well worth a visit.

Plate 22

View of the final approach to Snowdon summit showing Snowdon Railway extreme left. Pyg track right centre and Llanberis and lake top left.

Plate 23
Snowdon Mountain Railway with Llanberis in background

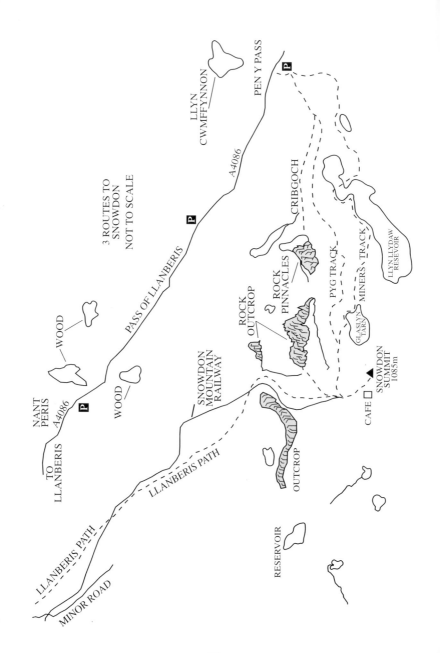

3 ROUTES TO SNOWDON
NOT TO SCALE

LLYN CWMFFYNNON

PEN Y PASS

A4086

PASS OF LLANBERIS

WOOD

NANT PERIS

A4086

TO LLANBERIS

WOOD

LLANBERIS PATH

SNOWDON MOUNTAIN RAILWAY

MINOR ROAD

LLANBERIS PATH

RESERVOIR

OUTCROP

ROCK OUTCROP

ROCK PINNACLES

CRIBGOCH

PYG TRACK

MINERS TRACK

GLASLYN TARN

LLYN LLYDAW RESEVOIR

SNOWDON SUMMIT 1085m

CAFE

70

SNOWDON

There are 2 main starting points to climb Snowdon on the 3 Peaks Walk. The Pyg Track is the easiest and most popular, the other is the Llanberis Path which ascends from the village of Llanberis.

Start A - The Pyg Track

Park at Pen-y-Pass car park opposite the youth hostel near the top of Llanberis Pass. This car park can be very busy, there is a charge for parking. Your ascent of Snowdon begins here.

Your path is in the upper right hand corner of the car park, continue on the path to a stone wall with an opening between. There are good views from here down the valley. You will see the narrow slate path in front of you. The path ascends a hill, it is very uneven with slabs of stone formed into steps. You can see the obvious path winding up the mountain, keep to this undulating path.

You come to some posts and a wire fence, there are good views of Crib Goch and a reservoir can be seen in the valley. As you look down in the valley you will see the Miners Track which is the alternative route back *(plate 20)*.

A slate chipping path winds round Crib Goch Coll. It starts to ascend as you are walking parallel with the small reservoir, you then look into the next part of the valley as you come over the coll. There is another small tarn in view, tucked into the valley floor *(plate 20)*. The path is very evident into the next part of the valley *(plate 18)*, directly across is Snowdon.

A large expanse of stone, sloping to your left is in front of you *(plate 21),* this can be very slippy when wet, boots are advised. You have a good view of the second tarn in front. When you round a large expanse of rock you see the third section of this path which is undulating.

There are veins of quartz in much of the rock formations, these look like snow from a distance. There are the occasional pile of stones on route. As you pass a cairn on your left the path is again scree.

Near the head of the valley is a small pool of water some 30m wide. About 70m further up there is part of a disused quarry on your left, the path bears off to the right.

The ascent now is steeper with a lot of loose stones and shale. You will see a monolith directly ahead of the zig-zag route *(plate 19).* At the head of this section there are large stone blocks to walk up. Although still ascending, the going is a little easier. From the summit ridge a water pipeline at the bottom of the valley can be seen.

The view once you attain the ridge looking towards Llanberis and in all directions is spectacular *(plate 20 & 22).* At the monolith you turn left joining the Llanberis Path for the final ascent. The path for the remaining distance to the summit is obvious, it runs parallel with the Snowdon Mountain Railway *(plate 23).* As you approach you will see the café with the triangulation pillar nearby.

You can go to the triangulation pillar for the customary photograph and viewing session. In the café there is time to relax over a variety of food and drinks while you look out and admire the views. A souvenir shop is next to the café.

You may wish to return to Pen-y-Pass via the Miners Track. This route takes you initially on a steep descent after leaving the Pyg Track *(plate 18)* then is virtually flat for the rest of the way back before becoming undulating in the last part. The return to Pen-y-Pass by this route is as follows:-

Retrace your steps to the monolith, go down the zig-zag path *(plate 19)*. Just past this you should see a stone/scree descent *(plate 18)* off to your right leading to Glaslyn Tarn. Follow this path to the bottom taking extreme care. Once at the bottom follow the well made track around the reservoir passing some ruined buildings on your left. Go over the causeway and past another tarn. This path will take you back to Pen-y-Pass.

This route is an enjoyable walk and takes approximately 1½ hours to return.

Start B - Llanberis Path

Park your vehicle in Llanberis and walk to the Royal Victoria Hotel near to the Snowdon Mountain Railway. Opposite there are a number of tourist signs. One points to Snowdon Path. Follow this along the road passing a row of houses. Cross the cattle grid at the far end and ascend the very steep metalled road to a holiday house just round a sharp bend. Continue through a metal swing gate onto a stone/shale path, still ascending steeply, to a sign pointing to Snowdon through a metal gate.

Ascend an obvious rough path. The first third ascends steeply as does the last third. This also has a lot of loose stone on it making walking difficult. The central section is on a slight ascent *(plate 17)*.

On the way up you pass under 2 small bridges carrying the Snowdon Mountain Railway. Throughout the summer you may see the trains going up and down the line. You pass a steel structure which was abandoned due to legal disputes during building. This is known as the halfway house and is a convenient refreshment stop being approximately halfway to the summit.

Stay on the obvious path right to the summit. The top half of the route is very exposed in wet and windy weather. Nearing the summit you come to a large stone monolith on your left. This is where the Pyg Track and Miners Track join in a final ascent to the summit *(plate 22)*.

Retrace your steps to return to Llanberis or alternatively descend on one of the other paths.

In the event of lost bearings or low clouds on the summit of Snowdon then follow the bad visibility descent to take you to safer ground *(plate 20)*.

Now you have conquered all 3 peaks of Scotland, England and Wales you can complete your challenge by driving to Caernarfon and touching the sea.

BAD VISIBILITY DESCENTS

During the ascent of any mountain care should be taken especially in bad visibility.

More accidents happen on the return journey than on the ascent. It may be difficult to pick out the path of descent in low cloud or in darkness. In situations like this follow the bearings and details below to ensure a safe descent from the summit.

Ben Nevis

Walk from the triangulation pillar on a **Grid Bearing** of **231°** for **150m.**

Follow a **Grid Bearing** of **281°** which should take you clear of the plateau onto your path.

Magnetic North is estimated at 5° W of Grid North in 1998 this decreases by about ½° every four years. The compass bearing is gained by adding this difference to the grid bearing, this is known as a magnetic bearing. Refer to current O.S. maps for magnetic variation.

Scafell Pike

Walk from the triangulation pillar on a **Grid Bearing** of **285°** for **200m**. Look carefully for the path and cairns.

Walk for **300m** on **Grid Bearing 345°**
Walk for **250m** on **Grid Bearing 318°**
Walk for **300m** on **Grid Bearing 252°**

Lingmell Col.

Dropping Crag

This route takes you to the left of Dropping Crag, down to Lingmell Col and around to Hollow Stones. In this area magnetic north is 4½° W of Grid North in 1999. The compass bearing is gained by adding this difference to the grid bearing. Refer to current O.S. maps for magnetic variation.

Following this course from the summit should bring you off the peak and below the rocks in front of the Pike itself. From this point you can follow the path downhill to Wastwater looking for the cairns on route.

Snowdon

Walk from the summit station/café on **Grid Bearing 334°** for **550m** following the distinct path. A railway line is on the left and a steep drop on the right. At the monolith turn right on **Grid Bearing 52°.** You are now on another distinct path going downhill. This path zig-zags sharply *(plate 19).* Stay on this path to descend, eventually leading back to Pen-y-Pass. In extreme bad weather follow the railway line down into Llanberis.

In the event of low cloud or other problem on the top half of the route, the Miners Track will take you to the valley quicker *(plate 18).* It starts about a third of the way down the mountain and branches off to the right. The path is steep at first but once at the bottom it is a good, virtually flat path to Pen-y-Pass. A sign is situated at the Pen-y-Pass end of this track giving current weather conditions.

In this area magnetic north is 4° W of Grid North in 1999 decreasing by about ½° in four years. The compass bearing is gained by adding the difference to the grid bearing. Refer to current O.S. maps for magnetic variation.

SUPPORT TEAM

When attempting the National 3 Peaks it is advisable to have a support team of 2-4 people who are able to drive between the 3 peaks and provide the food and drinks to tired walkers. It is not advisable for walkers to both attempt the 3 peaks and drive between each area. The general tiredness of driving the long distance between each mountain and the walker's fatigue makes it important to have a support team.

Providing food and warm drinks to walkers is very important especially in bad conditions. The last thing walkers need on returning to the foothills of each peak is to start preparing food and drinks. The assistance of a support team is therefore vital.

Members of any support team should have some knowledge of first aid and should be able to recognise the symptoms of exposure. They should be aware of the location of the mountain rescue posts and nearest telephone for emergency. The support team should keep a spare rucksack with the following inside:-

Map	Compass
Whistle	Emergency Food
Survival Bag	Notepad/Pencil
Spare Clothing	First Aid Kit
Matches	
Torch (spare bulb/batteries)	
Mobile Telephone (not guaranteed to function in mountainous areas)	

Where possible there should be two of the support team who are experienced and prepared to give assistance to any of the walkers in an accident/emergency situation. It may be decided that initially the best course of action is to go straight to the aid of a walker rather than contact the mountain rescue team. Any potential risks to both the injured or lost walker or the rescuer should be carefully considered before deciding your course of action.

POST WALK

After achieving your goal of walking the National 3 Peaks, whether it is in 24 hours or over a prolonged time, you may like a souvenir to mark the event. The author has produced a selection of items which are for sale. These are exclusive to Challenge Publications and include:- polo/t-shirts, cloth/metal badges, certificates for one or all peaks. Full details are available by sending for a current price list enclosing a S.A.E. to:-

Brian Smailes
Challenge Publications
7, Earlsmere Drive
Ardsley
Barnsley
South Yorkshire
S71 5HH

The author is compiling a register of successful attempts and would be pleased to receive any details and/or comments about your walk.

USEFUL INFORMATION

Heights of Peaks

Ben Nevis -1344 metres
Scafell Pike- 978 metres
Snowdon   - 1085 metres

Nearest Main Towns

Ben Nevis - Fort William
Scafell Pike- Keswick
Snowdon   - Llanberis

Nearest Telephone

Ben Nevis - Near Glen Nevis youth hostel
Scafell   - Wasdale Head Hotel
             - Nether Wasdale
             - Seathwaite
Snowdon   - Pen-y-Pass
             - Llanberis

Mountain Rescue Posts

Ben Nevis - Fort William town centre
Scafell   - Gatesgarth (Buttermere)
             - Wasdale Head
             - Mountain Rescue Kit near Sty
               Head on the Corridor Route
Snowdon   - Pen-y-Pass
             - Nant Peris in Pass of Llanberis

Recommended Maps

Ben Nevis - O.S. Outdoor Leisure No. 38
Ben Nevis & Glen Coe (1:25,000)

Scafell - O.S. Outdoor Leisure No.4 English
Lakes (1:25,000)
- O.S. Outdoor Leisure No.6 English
Lakes (1:25,000)

Snowdon - O.S. Outdoor Leisure No.17
Snowdonia (1:25,000)

Weatherline Service

Ben Nevis Area   0891 333198 (climb line)
Scafell Area   017687 75757
Snowdon Area   0891 500449

Grid References

Ben Nevis

Glen Nevis Visitor Centre   G.R. 123730
Glen Nevis Youth Hostel   G.R. 128718
Halfway point on main path, near Lochan
Lochan Meall An t-Suidhe   G.R. 147724
Emergency shelter, Ben Nevis summit
G.R. 167713

Beware, other shelter at G.R. 173714 above the Coire Leis as this involves very steep descents using abseil skills or use of the Carn Mor Dearg Arete.

Scafell Pike

Wastwater, Wasdale Head car park

	G.R. 182075
Base of Scafell Pike	G.R. 207074
Scafell Pike summit	G.R. 216072
Sty Head Tarn, Corridor Rte.	G.R. 221099

Seathwaite car park, Corridor Rte.

G.R. 235422

Snowdon

Pen-y-Pass youth hostel car park

	G.R. 647556
Snowdon summit	G.R. 610544
Start of Llanberis Path	G.R. 581595

Timing for each mountain

Ben Nevis

Youth Hostel start to summit	3½ hours
Summit to youth hostel	2½ hours

Scafell Pike

Wasdale Head start to summit	2¼ hours
Summit to Wasdale Head	2 hours
Seathwaite, start to summit	3½ hrs

Snowdon

Pen-y-Pass, Pyg Track start to summit	2¼ hours
Summit to Pen-y-Pass, via Miners Track	1½ hours
Llanberis Path to summit	2½ hours
Summit to Llanberis	1¾ hours

These timings will vary depending on the skill and fitness of your party e.g. Ben Nevis can be completed in 4½ hours with ease.

Suggested Itinerary

24 Hours Challenge
4pm   touch water - Fort William
4.30pm   start base of Ben Nevis
6.45pm   summit of Ben Nevis
8.30pm   base of Ben Nevis
2am   start base of Scafell Pike
4.45am   summit of Scafell Pike
6.15am   base of Scafell Pike
12.30pm   start base of Snowdon
2.30pm summit of Snowdon
3.30pm base of Snowdon
4pm touch water - Caernarfon

A Weekend Challenge
Saturday

start	4am	Glen Nevis Visitor Centre
	7.30am	Ben Nevis summit
	10am	Glen Nevis Visitor Centre
	6pm	Seathwaite-Lake District
	9.30pm	Scafell Pike summit
	11.30pm	Wasdale Head
	10am	Pen-y-Pass-Snowdon
	12.15pm	Snowdon summit

Sunday

finish	2pm	Pen-y-Pass car park

National Park/Tourist Information Centres

Glen Nevis Visitor Centre	01397 705922
Fort William T.I.C.	01397 703781
Keswick Information Centre	017687 72645
Seatoller Barn Info. Centre	017687 77294
Llanberis T.I.C.	01286 870765
Betws-y-Coed	01690 710426
Caernarfon	01286 672232

Accommodation-Ben Nevis area

Campsites

Glen Nevis Caravan & Camping Park	01397 702191
Lochy Caravan/Camping Park	01397 703446

Youth Hostels/Bunkhouses

Fort William Backpackers	01397 700711
Glen Nevis Youth Hostel	01397 702336
Glencoe Youth Hostel	01855 811219
The Smiddy Bunkhouse, Corpach, Fort William	01397 772467
Ben Nevis Bunkhouse	01397 702240
Calluna Bunkhouse	01397 700451

Bed & Breakfast

Glenlochy Guest House	01397 702909
Rhu Mhor Guest House	01397 702213
Achintee Farm	01397 702240
Mr. Fraser, Glen Nevis	01397 701436
Corrie Duff, Glen Nevis	01397 701412
Craig Nevis Guest House	01397 702023

Accommodation-Scafell Area

Campsites
Seathwaite Farm	017687 77284
Seatoller Farm	017687 77394
Stonethwaite	017687 77234
Wasdale Head, Barn Door Shop- (no showers)	019467 26384
Wasdale Head	019467 26220

Camping Barns/Youth Hostels
Seatoller Farm	017687 77394
Wasdale Hall Youth Hostel	019467 26222
Keswick Youth Hostel	017687 72484

Bed & Breakfast
Seathwaite Farm	017687 77284
Hollows Farm	017687 77298
Glaramara (Seatoller)	017687 77222
Burnthwaite Farm	019467 26242
Wasdale Head Hotel	019467 26229

Accommodation-Snowdon Area

Campsites
Dolgam, Capel Curig	01690 720228
Hafod Lydan, Llanberis	01286 870356
Ty Isaf, Nant Peris	01286 870494
Snowdon House, Nant Peris	01286 870718

Youth Hostels
Pen-y-Pass	01286 870428
Capel Curig	01690 720225
Llanberis	01286 870280

Bed & Breakfast

Marteg, Llanberis	01286 870207
Maesteg, Llanberis	01286 871187
Plas Coch, Llanberis	01286 872122
Bron-y-Graig, Llanberis	01286 872073

Attractions

Ben Nevis Area

Fort William Cruises	01397 703919
Nevis Range Cable Cars	01397 705825
Ben Nevis Distillery	01397 700200
Ben Nevis Woollen Mill	01397 704244
West Highland Museum	01397 702169
Lochaber Leisure Centre	01397 704359

Scafell Area

Lake Cruises on Windermere	015395 31188
Keswick Launch on Derwentwater	017687 72263
Motor Museum, Keswick	017687 73757
Cumberland Pencil Museum	017687 73626
'The Theatre by the Lake' Keswick	017687 74411

Snowdon Area

Snowdon Mountain Railway	01286 870223
Electric Mountain	01286 870636
Copper Mine	01766 510100
Padarn Country Park	01286 870892

Useful Addresses

Long Distance Walkers Association
Brian Smith
10 Temple Park Close, Leeds LS15 0JJ
Tel: 0113 2642205

This association is set up to further the interests of those who enjoy long distance walking. Members receive a journal three times each year which includes information on all aspects of long distance walking.

Ramblers Association
1-5 Wandsworth Road, London SW8 2XX

Advice and information on all walking matters. Local groups with regular meetings.

Snowdonia Society
Ty Hyll, Capel Curig,
Betws- y- Coed LL24 0DS
Tel: 01690 720287

GLOSSARY OF WORDS

Bearing - *A degree or number of degrees set on a compass, follow the direction of travel arrow walking on that bearing to reach your intended destination.*

Beck - *Cumbrian word for stream or brook.*

Burn - *Scottish word meaning stream, brook, beck or watercourse.*

Cairn - *An ancient stone mound erected as a marker. Often modern day piles of stones that denote a path or route are referred to as cairns.*

Col - *A pass or saddle between two hills. It provides access between one valley and another.*

Crag - *A steep rugged rock or peak.*

Escape Route - *Used for any emergency situation or in times of bad visibility. The main aim is to get you down to lower ground by the safest and quickest way.*

Glen - *Scottish word for a valley.*

Grid Reference - *Derived from the national grid reference system. This is used to pinpoint a place on a map by use of letters and numbers.*

Gully - *A narrow channel or cleft in a rock face, may have waterfalls and can be very slippery and have vertical drops.*

Kissing Gate - *Swing gate that usually lets one person through it at a time by moving the gate backwards and forwards.*

Loch - *Scottish word for lake.*

Magnetic Bearing - *This is a grid bearing taken from a map and the relevant magnetic variation added to it to obtain the magnetic bearing. See the relevant maps for details of current magnetic variation.*

Metalled Road - *Generally known as a stone chipping road. This term evolved and became regarded as the roads metal or the roads surface.*

Outcrop - *Part of a rock formation that sticks out from the main body of rock.*

Plateau - *A wide and mainly flat area of elevated land.*

Route Card - *A plan of action prepared before you leave. A copy to be left with someone so that if you fail to return by a planned time then help can be summoned.*

Summit - *The highest point of a mountain or hill.*

Tarn - *A small mountain lake.*

Trig Point - *True name is Triangulation Pillar. These mark the summit of many mountains but not all. It is a small stone pillar with a number on it. The height of the mountain is taken from this point.*

NOTES